JESU
AND HIM

GW01045873

D. Martyn Lloyd-Jones

Early in 1927 Dr Martyn Lloyd-Jones became the Minister of Bethlehem Forward Movement Mission Hall, Sandfields, Aberavon. On February 6th 1977, the fiftieth anniversary of the commencement of his ministry, he returned there and preached this sermon. It is reproduced here with an absolute minimum of editing.

THE BANNER OF TRUTH TRUST

THE BANNER OF TRUTH TRUST
3 Murrayfield Road, Edinburgh EH12 6EL
P.O. Box 621, Carlisle, Pennsylvania 17013, USA

*

First Published in *The Evangelical Magazine of Wales,* April 1981
First Banner of Truth edition 1999
ISBN 0 85151 780 3

*

Typeset in 10½/12pt Plantin Monotype
Printed in Great Britain by
Polton Press
Lasswade
Edinburgh

Jesus Christ and Him Crucified

'For I determined not to know any thing among you, save Jesus Christ, and him crucified' (1 Cor. 2:2).

I have a number of reasons for calling your attention tonight to this particular statement. One of them – and I think you will forgive me for it – is that it was actually the text I preached from on the first Sunday night I ever visited this church. That was not fifty years tonight, but fifty years on the 28th of November last year. My first visit here was on the 28th November, 1926, and the second verse of the second chapter of Paul's First Epistle to the Corinthians was my text at the evening service. Fifty years ago tonight, which was my first night here officially as minister, my text was 'God hath not given us the spirit of fear; but of power, and of love, and of a sound mind' (*2 Tim.* 1:7).

I call attention to my text not merely for that reason, but rather because it is still my determination. It is still what I am endeavouring to do, as God helps me. I preached on this text then – I have no idea what I said in detail, I have not got the notes – but I did so because it was an expression of my whole attitude towards life. It was what I felt was the commission that had been given to me. And I call attention to it again because it is still the same, and because I am profoundly convinced that this is what should control our every endeavour as Christian people and as members of the Christian church at this present time.

The foundation attacked

Now the apostle, as you remember, is dealing in these first chapters with the situation in the church at Corinth. And he reminds them here of how he first visited them, because there was no church in Corinth until the Apostle Paul went there and preached the gospel. The church came into being directly as the result of his preaching and his teaching. He established it, and it flourished.

But after a while other elements came in, and the church was in a very disturbed and unhappy condition when the apostle wrote this letter to them. That was why he wrote. He was concerned because things were being said and believed by some of them that were, in his opinion, attacking the very foundations of the gospel itself. So he reminded them of what he first preached and why and how he preached to them. And, as I say, I am calling attention to this because I feel it is equally important at the present time.

I need take none of your time in reminding you of the state of the world. We are living in a world of crisis and calamity. You never know what the next news bulletin is going to announce. It is a world which is in a state of collapse in almost every respect. It is a time of great trouble and perplexity. And the great question that arises is this: Has the Christian church anything to say at such a time? What has she got to say? What is the greatest need of the world tonight? What is the greatest need of every one of us, of every single human being? It is because I feel that, in these words, the great Apostle deals with and answers those very questions that I am calling attention to this great announcement, this great proclamation by him.

A solemn decision

You notice that he says that he 'determined not to know anything among them save Jesus Christ, and him crucified'. In other words, he had made a decision. It was something quite deliberate; it was not haphazard. His statement is that, having looked at the whole situation, he had come to a conclusion.

Now there are scholars who would have us believe that this decision was a kind of reaction to what had happened to the apostle in the great city of Athens. Those of you who are familiar with the history of the book of the Acts of the Apostles will remember that Paul went to Corinth from Athens after his preaching had been interrupted and his work had been unsuccessful. In his sermon in Athens, he had quoted some of the Greek poets. And these authorities tell us that Paul, having shown his knowledge of Greek literature and having more or less failed, said to himself on the road from Athens to Corinth, 'Well, I'd better not do that again.' And so he decided and determined not to know anything among them save Jesus Christ and him crucified.

Now I think that is entirely wrong. I reject that interpretation completely, because, after all, the mere quoting of some two poets was neither here nor there; it did not affect the thrust of his message. Paul preached Jesus Christ and him crucified in Athens quite as much as he did in Corinth. Indeed, this is what he did everywhere. He had decided at the very outset of his ministry that this was to be his great theme to the exclusion of everything else. This, then, was not an entirely new decision but was a repetition of his original resolve. But here Paul reminds the Corinthians of what he had actually done among them. He had come to this decision quite deliberately, because he could have done many other things. He was an unusually able and erudite man. So it was a very solemn decision.

Indeed, the Apostle goes further in the next two chapters. In chapter 3 he puts it like this: 'Let no man deceive himself. If any man among you seemeth to be wise in this world, let him become a fool, that he may be wise' (verse 18); and later he goes on to say that he had deliberately become a fool for Christ's sake. What he means by 'a fool' is, of course, someone who is regarded as an ignoramus by these Greeks. The Greeks were very able people, great philosophers, and the apostle knew perfectly well that if he preached only Jesus Christ and him crucified and did not preach philosophy and other things to them, they would dismiss him as an ignoramus and as a fool. And so he says, 'All right, I deliberately became a fool for Christ's sake'. So that is what he is clearly saying here – that he went out of his way, as it were, and deliberately decided that he would reject everything else and all other knowledge; and, in simplicity, as one regarded as a fool and a babbler by these learned people in Athens and in Corinth, that he would know nothing among them save Jesus Christ and him crucified.

He knew, as he has already told them in the first chapter, that his message was going to be a stumbling-block to the Jews, and that the Greeks would regard it as unutterable foolishness. He was a Jew himself, and he knew the Jewish attitude. He knew that this preaching of the cross was a real stumbling-block to the Jew, and that the Greeks regarded it as just nonsense. That a carpenter in a place like Palestine, by dying on a cross, should be the Saviour of the world – it was unutterable rubbish! He knew exactly what the Jews and the Greeks believed. Nevertheless, he decided deliberately that he would go on preaching it, in spite of the way in which they regarded it.

So let us be clear about this. This was a deliberate decision on the part of the great apostle. He 'determined not to know anything among them, save Jesus Christ and him crucified'.

Why this decision?

Well now, the question before us is this: Why did he come to this decision? Why did Paul resolve and determine to behave in this way? And, if I may say so with humility, why did I in my small way come to the same decision and the same determination? Or why am I, fifty years afterwards, still doing exactly the same thing? I cannot remember what I said fifty years ago, but I know that the thrust was the same. The essential message was the same, whatever the particular form and whatever the particular details might have been. Why did the apostle come to this decision? Why should every preacher of the gospel and the Christian church today come to this decision? I am convinced that the church is powerless today and is ignored by the people because she has not come to this decision – because she is doing the exact opposite and is trying to be all things to all men in a wrong way and in a wrong manner. So I regard it as very vital that we should be certain as to why the great apostle decided in this way. And I think he makes it abundantly plain to us as to why he did so.

The modern argument

Today, of course, the general view is almost the exact opposite of this. The argument is that if the church, the Christian church, is to have any impact upon people and is to win the people to the church and to Christ, well then, we must of necessity talk about things in which people are interested. That is the argument. It has been said throughout the centuries that it is no use going to men and women with their problems and difficulties of all sorts and kinds and just telling them about Jesus Christ and him crucified. They simply will not listen. You will have no impact at all. You will have a little coterie of people, perhaps, but it will have no widespread impact. If you want to influence people, we are told, and want to affect them and to win them, you must talk about the things in which they are interested.

Well now, there is nothing new about that. You see, that is exactly what they were saying nearly 2,000 years ago, when the great apostle visited Athens and Corinth. They always wanted any man who came to speak to talk about the things in which they were interested. You remember we are told about the people in Athens that they spent their time in doing 'nothing else, but either to tell, or to hear some new thing' (*Acts* 17:21). They were very fond of listening to people, and when Paul came along they said, 'What will this babbler say?' They were ready to listen. But they always wanted a man to speak about the things in which they were interested. What were they?

The law

Well, the people consisted partly of Jews and mainly, probably, of Greeks. What were they interested in? What did they want Paul to talk about? The answer, of course, is quite simple. The Jews were always interested in the law – the law given by God through Moses to the children of Israel. And they were always arguing and debating about it. 'Which is the most important element in the law, the first and the greatest commandment?' Nothing pleased the Jews more than to be arguing about the law and the respective merits of the particular commandments. And they were always ready to listen to a man who talked about it.

Philosophy

The Greeks – well, we know exactly what they were interested in. As I have already reminded you, the Greeks were primarily interested in what is called philosophy. I suppose in many ways the Greeks were the ablest, the most intelligent race of people that the world has ever known. It was the country which had produced the greatest succession of philosophers the world has ever known – Socrates, Plato, Aristotle. And they had all been teaching in Greece before Christ and Paul ever appeared on the scene. The Greeks were tremendously interested in this question of philosophy.

What does it mean? Well, philosophy means the attempt to understand life. You see, any intelligent man in a world

[8]

like ours, seeing the problems and the pain and the trouble, any intelligent man doesn't go and have a drink to forget all about it. He says, 'Why are things like this? What is the matter? Were we meant to be like this? Can anything be done about it?' So these Greeks with their great minds applied themselves to the study of the problem of life and living; and, of course, there were rival teachings and rival views. They all set up their so-called porches, academies if you like – what would now correspond to our universities and schools and so on – and there were the rival theories. You read about the Stoics and the Epicureans, and they put forward their views and argued as to how man might perhaps even arrive at Utopia, a perfect condition.

Culture

But again, another branch of philosophy was what is called culture. What do they mean by culture? Well, we all know about this. You have all, I am sure, watched those famous lectures by Lord Clark on the television – 'Civilisation'. Culture! They were expert architects, they built their magnificent buildings. You can still go and see the ruins in Athens, and it is worth a visit even to see the ruins – they were such magnificent buildings. General culture, architecture, monuments, all these things. The same was true of art. They were interested in art in every shape and form. And they delighted in and discussed these things. In addition to that, they were great experts on sport. We get excited about the Olympic Games. We did not start them, you know. It was they, the Greeks, who started the Olympic Games and they who named the Marathon race. These were the things which these intellectual people worked out and elaborated. This was the centre of their interest. They were concerned likewise about social conditions, about ethics and morality and all these matters.

Then the apostle came amongst them. He knew that these were the subjects in which they were interested, and that any man who talked about any one of these things was not only sure of interested hearers but might even become popular among them. Yet, knowing that these were the things that the people were interested in, and having the ability and the understanding to deal with them, this man deliberately decided and determined not to deal with any of those subjects. 'I determined not to know any thing among you save Jesus Christ and him crucified.'

They come to nought!

Well now then, the question is, 'Why did he decide that? Why did he determine that?' And fortunately for us, he gives us the answer in the sixth verse of this second chapter of First Corinthians, 'Howbeit', he says, 'we speak wisdom among them that are perfect: yet not the wisdom of this world, nor of the princes of this world, that come to nought.' Nought! Nothing! A cipher! Vacuity! Nothing at all! Why didn't Paul preach philosophy, why didn't he preach politics, why didn't he preach culture and art and all these things? The answer is, he says, they come to nothing. Nought!

Is he right? Well, let us test. Let us test by what he says himself in his epistles. Let us test by the history of the world.

What of this question of law that the Jews were so interested in? Why didn't the apostle preach perpetually on the details and the minutiae of the law, as the Pharisees had always done? Why didn't he spend the whole of his time in just expounding the law? He gives us the answer in many, many places. You have it, for instance, in the twentieth verse of the third chapter of his great Epistle to the Romans. 'Therefore by the deeds of the law there shall no flesh be justified in his sight: for by the law is the knowledge of sin' – and nothing else. The law will give you a knowledge of sin, and it will condemn you. But it will leave you grovelling in the dust. You have it again in Romans 8:3 – 'For what the law could not do, in that it was weak through the flesh, God sending his own Son in the likeness of sinful flesh, and for sin, condemned sin in the flesh.'

In other words, the law was a failure. Nobody could keep the law, the law about which these Jews and experts argued so much. It could not help men, it simply condemned them. It exposed the need and the ills, but it left them grovelling in the dust in complete hopelessness. I did not preach the law, says Paul, because it could not do anything for you. It comes to nought. It leaves you in utter helplessness.

And the same thing applies precisely and exactly to all these other questions. Why did not Paul preach philosophy? His answer is that it all comes to nothing. He calls it here human wisdom, the wisdom of this world. Do you know that before Christ ever came into this world, the greatest philosophers that the world has ever known had already been here? They had already given us their great teaching. They had put forward their plans and their proposals for Utopia. But it was all a failure. The statistics – they are not in the Bible, but they are in secular history – the statistics show that the rate of suicide was higher proportionately amongst the philosophers than any other single section of the community. Philosophy was failing. It had had its trial. God, as it were, had kept his Son back until human wisdom and learning had had their full opportunity. And Paul says it has come to nothing – 'the world by wisdom knew not God' (*1 Cor.*1:21).

Failure in the old world
It is all very well to raise questions, but you know a great man, Thomas Masaryk – the man who founded the state of Czechoslovakia after the end of the First World War – that great leader of Czechoslovakia put it like this: 'The philosophers have only interpreted the world in various ways.

The point, however, is to change it.' The philosophers were very clever in putting forward different points of view and different interpretations. But that leaves us where we are. What the world needs is to be changed. And no philosopher has ever changed this world. No, no! The old world, in spite of the teaching of these master thinkers and philosophers, was in a terrible state and condition.

What was it? Well, you need not take my word for it. The Apostle Paul has given us a description of it at the end of the first chapter of his Epistle to the Romans. This was the state of society. In spite of Greek philosophy and culture, Roman law, and all the politics of the age, this is how people were living. 'As they did not like to retain God in their knowledge, God gave them over to a reprobate mind, to do those things which are not convenient; being filled with all unrighteousness, fornication, wickedness, covetousness, maliciousness; full of envy, murder, debate, deceit, malignity; whisperers, backbiters, haters of God, despiteful, proud, boasters, inventors of evil things, disobedient to parents, without understanding, covenant-breakers, without natural affection, implacable, unmerciful: who knowing the judgment of God, that they which commit such things are worthy of death, not only do the same, but have pleasure in them that do them' (*Rom.* 1:28–32). That is how they were living, instead of according to the great teachings of the philosophers. Previously Paul has been telling us about the terrible, scandalous, sexual perversions – men leaving the right use of the woman and turning to men, dishonouring their own bodies between themselves. The whole world was a sink of iniquity. In spite of all the blueprints for Utopia, all the politics, all the social ameliorations that were being proposed, all the learned arguing and disputation of the philosophers, that is how they were actually living. Paul was right. All this comes to nothing. Nought! Failure! Nothing! Blank!

Failure today

And, my dear friends, as it was true then it is true today, and it has continued to be true throughout the centuries. People today are interested in the same things. We express it in different forms, but for a hundred years or more, people have been trusting to these things. People have stopped going to chapels and churches. Why? They have stopped believing the Bible. What do they believe in? Philosophy. The great philosophers. And you can hear them now whenever you like on the television and the radio. Philosophy! Politics! We were assured that politics was going to change the face of society. It was being preached here by Ramsay MacDonald and many another when I came here fifty years ago. This was what was going to put the world right – education, culture. Not such nonsense, such folk lore and fairy tales as the Bible and the Scriptures, but new knowledge, science, under-standing and philosophy – they were going to make a perfect world!

Now these are sheer facts. But what is the position? What has it all come to? I am here to remind you that what the apostle said in his day is equally true today. It comes to nought. It comes to nothing. Do not misunderstand me; there are particular benefits that we have all received, and we thank God for them. But face to face with the problem of man and of life and death and true living and peace and happiness and joy, they have all completely failed. They have come to nought.

Education fails

Now you need not take my word for this. Let me give you some quotations which will substantiate my contention. Take a great man like Tolstoy, Count Tolstoy, one of the greatest novelists of all times, the author of *War and Peace* and other masterpieces. Do you know what he said? Let me read his words to you. 'The meaningless absurdity of life is the only incontestable knowledge accessible to men.' The meaningless absurdity of life – that, he says, is the only thing which is incontestable.

But let me give you another. A man called Morris Ginsberg, who is an expert on sociology and political matters today, wrote quite recently: 'Modern psychological theories expose the naivety of the assumption which earlier theories have taken for granted, namely, that intellectual advance will be necessarily reflected in improved human relationships.' That was the assumption of our fathers, grandfathers and fore-fathers. They assumed that intellectual advance would of necessity be reflected in improved human relationships. Is that so? Has it happened? Are human relationships better? This was the assumption: give people knowledge and intellectual advance, and human relationships will be better.

But come, last year, 1976, was the centenary of the birth of a man called Albert Mansbridge. And I refer to Albert Mansbridge for this reason. Here was the man who started the Workers' Educational Association – the WEA. I do not know whether WEA classes are popular here now; they were very popular fifty years ago, and many people had left the churches and the chapels believing they were going to find salvation in the WEA classes. What had Albert Mansbridge said? He started these WEA classes in 1903, and what he said was this – and he really believed it, there was never a more honest, earnest and sincere man; he really believed it, and he made sacrifices for it – 'If enough effort', he said in 1903, 'was put into the education of the workers, then the main social problems of this present age would solve themselves.' That is what he believed, and thousands believed it with him. If only people put an effort into education, and if only the masses of the people were educated, the main social problems of the age would solve themselves. They put it into practice, and men really believed that if only we could all be educated we would solve all our problems.

What has it come to, my friends? Are there no social problems in Aberavon, Port Talbot, tonight? Are they much less than they were one hundred years ago or fifty years ago? I leave you to answer the question.

Moral inability

Come, let me give you another – Professor Arnold Toynbee, a great historian, published his massive *History of the World* in ten volumes, eventually twelve volumes. His last book bore the title *Mankind and Mother Earth*, and it was published last year. Now here is a man who spent a lifetime studying the human condition, trying to understand life and the world from the standpoint of history, not merely as an academic exercise, but because he wanted to make a contribution. He wanted things to be better and to be improved. But this is what he said in his last book, when he was an old man: 'There is a morality gap in the development of mankind. Man constantly extends his physical power over the environment, but he is unable to improve his social arrangements correspondingly; still less to subdue his destructive passions. Technology is the only field of human activity in which there has been progression.' That is Arnold Toynbee. He was not a Christian; he was a humanist. He did not believe this gospel of Jesus Christ and him crucified. He was a man who believed these various ideas – philosophy and so on – but he maintains that the only development that there has been is in the realm of technology.

We can certainly land people on the surface of the moon, but are we living any better? Has there been corresponding advance in the matter of man's social arrangements? Do we know how to subdue man's destructive passions? Oh, the brilliant technology of the last few years, conquering the force of gravity, landing men on the surface of the moon! Marvellous, wonderful! Has it lessened the destructive capacity of man and the destructive desires of man? Well, I ask you to look around you, read the newspapers, listen to the bulletins on the news. These men, who are not Christians at all, by simply viewing the facts and facing them squarely, have come to the conclusion that it all comes to nought.

No answers

I end with a quotation from Mr Aldous Huxley. Here was a brilliant man, a brilliant novelist, who believed in what is called Scientific Humanism for so many years and wrote about it in his novels. He came to feel that that was not the answer, and then he turned to mysticism and became a Buddhist. But still he was not satisfied, and if you read his biography you will find that he said this at the end of his life. Now again, here is a man who really was concerned about men and women and life and living. He wanted to live a better life himself. He wanted the world to be a better place. He was appalled at the two world wars, the making of the atomic and the hydrogen bombs. He was aghast at it all and had spent a lifetime trying to understand it. But this is what he said at the end of his life : 'It is a bit embarrassing to have been concerned with the human problem all one's life and that at the end one has no more to offer by way of advice than "Try to be a little kinder".' After all the brilliant philosophy and scientific reasoning, this is all he has got to tell us: 'Try to be a little kinder.'

Total bankruptcy

These men who were going to solve the problems – education, knowledge, culture, philosophy, politics – and who were going to put the world right, this is what they have to admit at the end. Well now, you see, they are but confirming what the great apostle tells us in the sixth verse of this second chapter of the First Epistle to the Corinthians. He says: 'I've got a wisdom, but it isn't a wisdom of this world – the thing you want me to be talking about. Why am

I not talking about it? I'll tell you. It comes to nothing. It's a blank, it's a cipher. It leaves you at the end with nothing at all. Just "try to be a little kinder"! What a bankruptcy! What a complete failure!'

And this is what the world needs to be told tonight: that all it has trusted to, and the men it has trusted, have led them to the present chaos, and have nothing to offer us, and have no hope. They make promises, but who believes them? They do not believe them themselves. They have been falsified. They are baffled, they are bewildered, they do not know where they are. It comes to nothing. Blank. Cipher. Vacuity. Complete hopelessness. Final despair.

Well there, my friends, I have taken the trouble to take you through all that, because the negative is important. People will not listen to the gospel until they have seen through the fallacy of everything else and the final uselessness of everything else.

But I cannot leave you on a negative. Let me come to the positive. 'I determined not to know anything among you' – none of those things. Why not? – 'but Jesus Christ and him crucified.' Why does he preach this? Why should every preacher of the gospel preach this? Why should the church today be telling the whole world that we need to be told about this – Jesus Christ and him crucified? Why did Paul determine to preach this?

A great commission
Here are some of the answers. The first was that he had been commanded to preach it. He had been given a commission. You remember the story? Saul of Tarsus, the Pharisee, the persecutor of Christians, going down from Jerusalem to Damascus breathing out threatenings and slaughter, going to exterminate the Christians. Suddenly he saw the light, and the face, and the voice which said,

'Saul, Saul, why persecutest thou me?. . . It is hard for thee to kick against the pricks.'

'Who art thou Lord?' he said; and he was told, 'I am Jesus whom thou persecutest.'

And he was given a great commission. He had become a new man, and the commission was this, that he should be a minister and a witness. Christ, the risen Christ, told him on the road to Damascus that he was to be a preacher of this gospel and that he was to proclaim him and him crucified to the people. So the apostle determines not to know anything among them because that is what he was called to preach.

You know, this is a matter of common honesty. The great apostle says elsewhere, 'I am an ambassador for Christ.' What is the business of an ambassador? Is it to voice his own opinions? Is it to say what he thinks? Well, if he does so, he is a very bad ambassador. The ambassador's job is to convey the thinking and the point of view of the country that has appointed him and which he is representing. He may disagree with it entirely, but it does not matter. The business of the ambassador is to deliver the message which has been given to him, to hand on this commission, whatever it is. And Paul says, I have no choice about this; that's what he told me to say. I'm not here to give you my theories and my ideas, he says. I am determined simply to preach what he gave me.

You notice, those of you who still read his epistles – and if you do not, you know, you are missing the greatest literature in the whole world – he talks about the deposit, the deposit that had been given to him, the dispensation of the gospel. 'I delivered unto you first of all' – what? what I thought, and what I had worked out philosophically? Oh, no! – 'that which I also received.' Revelation! The commission! The commandment! So simple, ordinary, common honesty dictated that the apostle should preach the message that he had been sent and commissioned to preach.

The testimony of God

But that is not the only reason by any means. Why did Paul only preach this? Well, he tells us again. 'And I, brethren, when I came to you, came not with excellency of speech or of wisdom, declaring unto you the testimony of God.' Later on he puts it like this: 'God hath revealed them unto us by his Spirit: for the Spirit searcheth all things, yea, the deep things of God' (verse 10). Why did Paul not preach politics and art and culture and philosophy? It was because he had a message about the deep things of God, the testimony of God. He says, 'You know, what I have preached to you was not man's ideas about the world and about life, but God's ideas!'

How can we waste our breath and our energy in preaching human ideas that come to nothing, when we have here what has been revealed to us, namely, God's view of it all? My dear friends, aren't you rather tired of listening to men – the most learned men – on the television, the radio, and everywhere else? They are very clever and expert at putting their points of view, and they speak with a rare dogmatism, making statements that they cannot prove and verify. Aren't you getting rather tired of listening to what men have to say? What is the greatest need in the world tonight? The greatest need of the world tonight is this: What has God got to say about it all?

Here is the question. Why is the world as it is? We have had two world wars in one century, haven't we? We had had one when I came here fifty years ago; we have had one since. We all know about these bombs. We have seen the breakdown of society. What is the matter? We know that acts of Parliament cannot put us right. We have had many of them, and they are tumbling out one after another, but the problems seem to increase instead of to lessen. What is the matter with the world? What is the matter with man? What is the matter with every one of us, individually and separately?

You know, my friends, there is only one satisfactory answer to that question. It is God's answer! It is God's answer! Why is the world as it is?

The answer, according to the Bible – Paul preached it everywhere – is this: that though God had made a perfect world, and had made man in a perfect condition and put him into Paradise where there were no problems and no difficulties, man's world is as it is tonight because man in his folly and his arrogance rebelled against God. He pitted his own mind against God. He did not care what God said. 'Ah, this is what I say,' he said. And he brought chaos upon himself, he was driven out of the garden, and he has been outside ever since, trying to get back. He cannot get back, and his world is in a muddle and in chaos. But God has given us the explanation. Why have we had the two world wars? Why may we have another? Why is society collapsing before our eyes? Why the immorality and the vice, the confusion, the unhappiness, the drug addiction and the alcoholism? Why the mounting social and moral problem? What is the explanation? Here it is. It is the only answer – man is estranged from God.

The wrath of God

But not only that. Man is under the wrath of God. This is what Paul preached. You remember how he put it in writing to the Romans: 'I am not ashamed of the gospel of Christ: for it is the power of God unto salvation to every one that believeth; to the Jew first, and also to the Greek. For therein is the righteousness of God revealed from faith to faith: as it is written, The just shall live by faith.' Then he goes on, 'For' – because – 'the wrath of God has [already] been revealed against all ungodliness and unrighteousness of men, who hold [down] the truth in unrighteousness' (*Rom.* 1:16–18). He says, That is why I am proud of the gospel. That is why I am so glad to preach it and consider it an honour to preach it. It is because it is the only hope for people who are under the wrath of God.'

And you know, my friends, this is the trouble with the world tonight. This world of ours is under the wrath of God. It is the only explanation of this twentieth century. In spite of all our education and culture and philosophy and politics and all that we have done, the world is in an increasing muddle. Why? Well, because God hates the way the world is living. He has always said so. God said through an Old Testament prophet 'There is no peace, saith my God, to the wicked' (*Isa.* 57:21). And this is the explanation of the world tonight. You can have a pocket full of money, you can have knowledge, you can have learning, you can have anything you like. But 'There is no peace, saith my God, to the wicked' – and they haven't got it! They have the money, many of them, and the learning and the knowledge, but they haven't got peace.

'The way of transgressors is hard' (*Prov.* 13:15) – and it is! Look at your modern world. It is hard, it is unhappy. The world is so unhappy that it has to turn to drugs and to alcohol. Men cannot go on without them, they are in such a desperate condition. Why is this? It is God's wrath upon us. God is not blessing us, and God will not allow us to be happy if we continue in a state of rebellion against him. As he demolished the tower of Babel, he is demolishing our towers of Babel, the things in which we put our faith and our trust. The things that were the confidence of the Victorians – God has smashed them. Man shall not be happy while he is a rebel against God. The wrath of God has been revealed from heaven. It has been revealed tonight, and it is the only explanation of the state of the world at this moment.

Have you listened?

I have something much profounder to preach to you than politics. The politicians do not understand the state of the world tonight; they are fumbling. All their prophecies have been falsified. And all those who put their faith in these things do not know where they are. Poor H. G. Wells, with all his morals and his scientific knowledge! Do you know the title of his last book? *Mind at the End of Its Tether*. He did not understand it, he did not know what was happening. But the answer is that God looks down with displeasure upon us. He has made us; we are not our own; we are his creatures, and we were meant to live to his glory and to his honour. Until we do, we will never know peace, we will never know happiness, we will never know joy.

'I didn't preach those other things to you', says Paul, 'because I have the testimony of God to preach to you. I wanted to tell you about the deep things of God.'

This analysis of God on the human situation – aren't you ready to listen to it? Aren't you tired of the vain speeches of men? My dear friends, have you listened to God's diagnosis of your condition and the condition of the whole world?

God's solution
But again, I thank God that he did not stop at the negative – and I must not. That is God's diagnosis of the state of affairs. But, thank God, Paul was able to preach to them God's solution to our problems. Where everything else has failed to provide a solution, Paul says, 'We speak the wisdom of God in a mystery, even the hidden wisdom, which God ordained before the world unto our glory' (verse 6).

This is the solution. Are you hopeful about the future? Are you happy about the future prospects? What do you feel, if you do look ahead to the remainder of your life and on to your death? What have you got? Is there any hope? There is none! But, you know, here – and this is why Paul preached it and determined not to know anything else – here is God's plan for the salvation of the individual and of the whole world. God's plan of salvation, prepared and ordained before the very foundation of the world, but now put into practice.

What is this? What is God's plan for this world? Well, you see, it is the exact antithesis of all human proposals. The world is always waiting for some great man – great men of history. And if there is any crisis, we hope a great man is going to emerge. Have you read these journalists? They often say this. This always happens, you know, when we face a terrible crisis, 'the great man' always appears on the scene – and they mention the great men. This is the way the world always looks at this.

Is that God's plan? Thank God it isn't. 'I determined not to know anything among you, save Jesus Christ.' Who is this? Well, he is a man, Jesus of Nazareth, a carpenter – a great man! Well, is this the answer? No, says Paul, listen! You must know who he is – 'which none of the princes of this world knew'. They thought he was only a man – 'for had they known it, they would not have crucified the Lord of glory'. Here is God's solution. My dear people, this is why I rejoice in this gospel. It is the only answer. 'God so loved the world that he gave' – a great philosopher? A great politician? – 'He gave his only begotten Son', Jesus of Nazareth, the Lord of glory. Paul, as I reminded you, came to this realization on the road to Damascus. He had regarded this Jesus as a carpenter and had dismissed him and derided him. He had blasphemed him. But on the road to Damascus, he discovered that the despised Jesus is the Lord of glory, the second Person in the blessed Holy Trinity, and that he had been in this world because God his Father had sent him. This is God's way of salvation.

It is the great message of the incarnation, and it is literally the only hope. Everything man does is a failure. But God has sent his own Son – the miracle, the mystery, the marvel of the incarnation, a little babe was born in a stable in Bethlehem! Why was he born in a stable? 'Because there was no room for them in the inn.' Oh, the people with money had booked the rooms! They are not going to turn out because a poor pregnant woman on the verge of giving birth to a baby has arrived. Why should they give up their rooms? They were as selfish then as people are today – pushing themselves forward in the queue, asserting their rights, not caring about anything as long as they are all right. A babe was born in a stable amidst the straw and the lowing of the cattle, a little helpless babe, and they put him into a manger. Who is this? The Lord of glory!

> *Veiled in flesh the Godhead see!*
> *Hail, the incarnate Deity!*

This is what Paul preached. 'God hath visited and redeemed his people.' God has come into time. God has sent his own Son. He had raised great prophets, great servants; they had all failed. But now he sends his only Son. So Paul preached Jesus Christ to them, showing them that he was none other than the eternal Son of God and the Lord of glory. This was proved by his miracles. It was proved by his life and by his teaching, his perfect example. But above all it was proved by his conquest over all the devils and everything that assails man. It was proved by his conquest of the tempest, the raging of the sea, the storm – the Lord of creation! And supremely it was proved by his glorious resurrection, when he even burst asunder the bands of death and arose triumphant over the grave. Jesus Christ!

My friends, are you interested in this Person? Do you know that God has intervened about our state and about our condition, and that he has come in the Person of his own Son? God has come in the flesh, 'in the likeness of sinful flesh and for sin'. Talk about Plato and Socrates? No, no! When I can talk about Jesus Christ, I cannot talk about them. Why talk about men when you can speak of the Lord of glory? That is why Paul determined not to know anything among them but Jesus Christ, and him crucified.

[24]

And this addition is essential: the cross, Calvary – this thing that is a stumbling-block to the Jews and utter foolishness to the Greeks. All right, you say, miracles are all right; but he died in utter weakness. Why didn't he come down and save himself? He died an ignominious death, a death of shame, and they buried him in a tomb. Why emphasize 'him crucified'? And the apostle tells us. He tells us, 'We preach Christ crucified, unto the Jews a stumbling-block and unto the Greeks foolishness, but unto them which are called, both Jews and Greeks, Christ the power of God, and the wisdom of God.'

Be reconciled to God

What does it mean? Let me hurriedly summarize it. Your greatest need and mine – the greatest need of the whole world – is to be reconciled to God. Nothing can avail us but that we are reconciled to God. All our troubles are due to the fact that we are aliens and rebels and, as I say, under the curse and the wrath of God. Man's supreme need is to be right with God and to be blessed by God.

How can it happen? Here are my sins and they come between me and God. I cannot get rid of them. What I have done I have done, and if I spent an eternity trying to erase my sins, I cannot do it.

> *Not the labours of my hands*
> *Can fulfil Thy law's demands;*
> *Could my zeal no respite know,*
> *Could my tears forever flow,*
> *All for sin could not atone:*

– it is impossible! –

> *Thou must save, and Thou alone.*

And he has done it in Jesus Christ and him crucified. The meaning of the death on the cross is this: God being holy, cannot pretend that he has not seen sin. He is a just and a righteous and a holy God, and he has said that 'the soul that

[25]

sinneth, it shall die.' 'The wages of sin is death' – and it is evident in the modern world.

Very well, how can I be reconciled to God? What can be done about my sins? God has said he must punish them. His righteousness demands it. But if he punished my sins, it would be the end of me. I would go to eternal death.

But God has planned a way, and he planned it before the very foundation of the world. He sent his own Son, spotless, pure, undefiled, who had never broken an iota of the law, who had given his Father complete obedience. God sent him to the cross, and he laid our sins upon him. 'He hath made him to be sin for us, who knew no sin; that we might be made the righteousness of God in him.' 'God was in Christ' – in and through Christ, and particularly on the cross – 'reconciling the world unto himself, not imputing their trespasses unto them' (*2 Cor.* 5:21,19). Or as Peter puts it, 'who his own self bare our sins in his own body on the tree, that we, being dead to sins, should live unto righteousness: by whose stripes ye were healed' (*1 Pet.* 2:24).

My dear friends, the only way of being reconciled to God is to know that Christ has died for your sins, borne your punishment, borne your guilt. In him you are reconciled to God. And so Paul preached Jesus Christ and him crucified.

God's power at work

And then, to round it off: Paul preached this and nothing else because it is the only thing that works. Nothing else works. We have seen the failure. This works. This is the power of God as well as the wisdom of God. And as the apostle says, 'Eye hath not seen, nor ear heard, neither have entered into the heart of man, the things which God hath prepared for them that love him' (verse 9). 'Jesus Christ and him crucified.' Why? Because it works and because of the things that it gives us.

What does it give us? It gives me a knowledge of sins forgiven. What a wonderful thing it is to have your conscience cleared! You may have done terrible things, and you cannot forgive yourself, and you are afraid to die – and rightly so, because when we die we all have to stand before God in judgment. How can I get rid of these sins? How can I know my sins are forgiven? There is only one answer. It is in Jesus Christ and him crucified. 'Being justified by faith, we have peace with God through our Lord Jesus Christ' (*Rom.* 5:1). What a wonderful thing it is to know that your sins are forgiven! – that you can put your head on the pillow and not worry as to whether you will ever wake up or not! You know that you are right with God, you are at peace with God; nothing can ever separate you from the love of God. My friends, have you got peace? Have you got peace of conscience? Are you ready to face death? Are you ready to face judgment? This is the only way. But it is given to us: 'the things that are freely given to us of God' (verse 12).

This is Christianity. Not an exhortation to you to go home and turn over a new leaf and try and live a better life. No, no! Come as you are – without money and without price.

> *Only believe, and thou shalt see*
> *That Christ is all in all to thee.*

It is the gift of God. 'By grace are ye saved through faith; and that not of yourselves: it is the gift of God' (*Eph.* 2:8). So you have forgiveness, peace with God, reconciliation with God, peace within, an understanding of life, a new outlook, a new understanding of other people. You have got a new life in you. And you begin to know joy that the world can never know and never has known, a joy that will hold and last whatever may be happening to you. Paul in writing to the Romans says, 'We glory in tribulations also.'

> *When all things seem against us,*
> *To drive us to despair,*
> *We know one gate is open,*
> *One ear will hear our prayer.*

A vision of glory

And, above it all, a vision of a glory that is to come. This old world – it is in terrible trouble, and according to the teaching of Christ and this man Paul, it is going to get worse and worse. 'Evil men shall wax worse and worse.' There will be wars and rumours of wars. Christianity has never promised to make this old world perfect in that way and to banish war. That is not Christianity: that is humanism. Christianity says that while men and women remain rebellious against God, the misery will increase and things will become terrible.

But the Christian, the man that believes in Jesus Christ and in him crucified, knows that a part of God's plan is this: that at some future date (we do not know when) God is going to send his Son, Jesus Christ, the Lord of glory, back to this world again. And he will come riding the clouds of heaven surrounded by the holy angels; he will come 'conquering and to conquer'. He will judge the whole world in righteousness. All the evil and sin and the chicanery and the dishonesty and the foulness of the perversions, and the way people are living today, it will all be dashed to a lake of perdition with all who have belonged to it and who have rejected this message. He will purge the whole universe of it all, and there shall be a 'new heavens and a new earth, wherein dwelleth righteousness.'

The Christian is not afraid of life, he is not afraid of death. He knows that there is a glory. Christ at the end of his life came to his disciples and said, 'Let not your heart be troubled: ye believe in God, believe also in me. In my Father's house are many mansions: if it were not so, I would have told you. I go to prepare a place for you. And if I go and prepare a place for you, I will come again, and receive you unto myself; that where I am, there ye may be also' (*John* 14:1–3). This is it. Whatever happens to us, whatever this old world may do, if they let off their bombs and if hell rages, it does not matter! Nothing 'shall be able to separate us from the love of God, which is in Christ Jesus our Lord.'

That is why Paul determined not to know anything among them, save Jesus Christ and him crucified. He had come to know this blessed Person. He had begun to receive of the riches of his grace, these things that God had prepared for them that love him, and he was rejoicing in them. It had worked! It is a power! He had been a miserable sinner, a Pharisee, self-righteous, self-contained, religious, moral, but miserable. But now he knows a joy unspeakable and full of glory. He looks and longs for this great day, when his Lord of glory shall come and every eye shall see him, and those that have believed in him shall be changed into his likeness. Their very bodies shall be changed, and they will live with him and reign with him, and spend their glorious eternity with him.

That is why Paul preached Jesus Christ and him crucified to the exclusion of everything else. It had worked in his life. It had made a new man of him. It had given him all this.

Men made new
But it had not only done it to Paul; it had done it, you know, to some of these people in Corinth. Listen to this in chapter 6. 'Know ye not that the unrighteous shall not inherit the kingdom of God? Be not deceived: neither fornicators, nor idolaters, nor adulterers, nor effeminate, nor abusers of themselves with mankind, nor thieves, nor covetous, nor drunkards, nor revilers, nor extortioners, shall inherit the kingdom of God. And such were some of you: but ye are washed, but ye are sanctified, but ye are justified in the name of the Lord Jesus, and by the Spirit of our God' (6:9–11).

Here were men, now members of the church at Corinth, who once had been dock labourers and other things in the dock yards and in the harbour at Corinth. They were drunkards, they were revilers, they were all these things.

Great philosophy had been preached. It did not touch them! They were there – besotted drunkards, guilty of all these offences and these obscenities. Nothing could touch them. Nothing could improve them. Neither philosophy, nor politics, nor sociology, nor education, nor anything! But such were some of you! You are no longer that. You have been washed.

> *There is power, power, wonder-working power*
> *In the precious blood of the Lamb.*

The preaching of Jesus Christ and him crucified 'in demonstration of the Spirit and of power' had raised these men up. It had renovated them, and they were saints adorning the church of God.

I cannot refrain from saying it. This not only works with Paul, it not only worked with these people in Corinth, it has worked in this very room in Sandfields, Aberavon. 'Such were some of you.' I could name them to you. Some of you have heard their names. Did you ever hear of a man called William Thomas, otherwise known as Billy Fair-play, Billy Staffordshire? He spent a lifetime in drunkenness, fighting, debauchery, hopelessness – until he was 77 years of age. But one night in this very building he became a new man, he was washed, he was sanctified, he was justified. He became a saint. And Mr. E. T. Rees and I here had the great privilege of seeing him going from time to eternity with the face of an angel, shining, and holding out his arms evidently to this Lord of glory, who was waiting to receive him.

What nothing else could do, Jesus Christ and him crucified had done to him – and he was only one of many. I could mention them to you. I must not do so, but I could go on for hours, telling you of men and women with whom everything had failed, but who, believing in Jesus Christ and him crucified, had started a new life. And you know at this moment they are in the glory everlasting. We are surrounded by so great a cloud of witnesses.

Nothing else matters

Men and women, is Jesus Christ and him crucified everything to you? This is the question. It is a personal matter. Is he central? Does he come before anything and everything? Do you pin your faith in him and in him alone? Nothing else works. He works! I stand here because I can testify to the same thing.

> *E'er since, by faith, I saw the stream*
> *Thy flowing wounds supply,*
> *Redeeming love has been my theme,*
> *And shall be till I die.*

'God forbid that I should glory, save in the cross of our Lord Jesus Christ, by whom the world is crucified unto me, and I [crucified] unto the world' (*Gal.* 6:14).

My dear friends, in the midst of life we are in death. This is not theory; this is personal, this is practical. How are you living? Are you happy? Are you satisfied? How do you face the future? Are you alarmed? Terrified? How do you face death? You have got to die. Think of the people who were here fifty years ago. They are no longer here. Most of them have gone. We are all moving. 'Here have we no continuing city'; but can you say, 'We seek one to come'? Are you fixed entirely upon him – Jesus Christ, Lord of glory, Son of God, Saviour of the world, Jesus Christ and him crucified?

My dear friends, nothing else matters finally but this. All else will come to nought. This place has been much more affluent than it was when I was here. We had men here, you know, earning 37/6d. of the old money per week, but they were great saints. They have gone on to the glory. You have more money. You have had many things which were not here then. But it will all come to an end. You cannot take any of these things with you when you come to die. 'Naked came I out of my mother's womb, and naked shall I return thither' (*Job* 1:21). What will you have when that end comes? You will have nothing, unless you have Jesus Christ and him crucified. And having him, you will be able to say with Charles Wesley – we have already been singing it –

> *Thou, O Christ, art all I want;*
> *More than all in Thee I find; . . .*
>
> *Plenteous grace with Thee is found,*
> *Grace to cover all my sin;*
> *Let the healing streams abound,*
> *Make me, keep me pure within.*

Jesus Christ and him crucified! Do you know him? Have you believed in him? Do you see that he alone can avail you in life, in death, and to all eternity? If not, make certain tonight. Fall at his feet. He will receive you, and he will make you a new man or a new woman. He will give you a new life. He will wash you. He will cleanse you. He will renovate you. He will regenerate you, and you will become a saint, and you will follow after that glorious company of saints that have left this very place and are now basking in the sunshine of his face in the glory everlasting. Make certain of it, ere it be too late!

Let us pray.

O Lord our God, how can we thank thee that in a world of darkness and of sin and of shame there is this one and only light still shining, Jesus Christ and him crucified. God, open the eyes of all who do not know him and have not seen him. Have mercy. Unstop deaf ears. Open blind eyes. God save the people. Awaken them to their need and to the perfect provision that thou hast made in the Son of thy love, the Lord of glory. And unto thee and unto thee alone shall we give all the praise and all the honour and all the glory, both now and for ever. Amen.